I see my love more clearly
from a distance

I see my love more clearly from a distance

Nora Gould

Brick Books

Library and Archives Canada Cataloguing in Publication

Gould, Nora, 1959-
    I see my love more clearly from a distance / Nora Gould.

Poems.
ISBN 978-1-926829-75-3

I. Title.

PS8613.O914I84 2012   C811'.6   C2011-908122-9

We acknowledge the Canada Council for the Arts, the Government
of Canada through the Canada Book Fund, and the Ontario Arts
Council for their support of our publishing program.

The pressed plant images on the cover and throughout the book are
photographs by Shannon R. White.

The author photograph was taken by Danielle Schaub.

The book is set in Minion and Mendoza.

Design and layout by Alan Siu.

Printed and bound by Sunville Printco Inc.

Brick Books
431 Boler Road, Box 20081
London, Ontario N6K 4G6

www.brickbooks.ca

Contents

I

II

III

IV

I

Every moon is perfect

His hand on my back, one finger lifts,
falls, on my scapula.

But it's her he holds in his sleep, dreams in his hands, Prairie,
his knee, his shoulder, his hands in her hair.

Under a perfect moon he doesn't speak my name.

Who can tilt the waterskins of the heavens?

Before ink, lithe with buffalo grass, rough
fescue, she came in season when old woman untied
Orion's belt and he flung aside his club. Prairie turned
with him, his hip, his shoulder, his sword
deep in her coulee. She held his seed
through many seasons, mule deer and whitetails
taking theirs in autumn when his constellation

rose in the east at sunset.
Now, pipes in sections, each joint rigid,
drilled deep in her parenchyma, have shifted, mixed
her fluids, frayed, broken her. Her hills
cut down, long scars converge
where flares stillbirth her northern lights

into sorrow. Sorrow, in the silences between her
measured phrases, she tastes air-
borne emissions, switches from her native

tongue. Frac fluid benzene H_2S sulphur
dioxide cannot be spoken with coneflower,
ascending milk-vetch; drilling mud with scarlet

mallow. Prairie turns to Orion, toluene blue
in his blood, his fluids
in her, her blood
loose in her body. Come morning, my cheek
on goat's flank, I taste lightning:

milk snow-blinds me. I, the goat, fuse.
Thunder cleaves an imperfect fissure.
Prairie's horizon is circled by mirage, flat-topped
cliffs where old woman, Breath, sits cross-legged.

Escher's spiral rotation of seasons

His sorrel mare keyed him in, was the spurtle
that stirred a lithograph of cows and calves
at dawn. Charl posted the trot, his boots

skimming alfalfa purples that goated around
my knees, soaked my thighs, pulled through
the arch of my jeans. I was on my shanks' pony,
my shoulders sweet clover damp.

Hazel, untethered by his whistle,
glistened out to gather strays.

Fox on hind legs, head above the barley,

watched the gliding reflection of cattle.
There was a translation of corvids: raven
for crow, a shift of buteos: Rough-legged
for Red-tailed. Snow betrayed the mouse,
lined every trail through the buckbrush,
along the side hill. Every path

led to water.
On Waldron's, cattle clustered
around the truck, bawling. In the dugout
not even mud for a cow to die in, the creek
dry on Lewsaw's. Charl hauled water
makeshift, the Chev top heavy, grasshoppers
raining on the windshield. Five hours
hauling water every day and the wondering:
where to move the cows next.

                    I closed my eyes,
my breasts browsed Charl's back,

my mouth grazed along his spine.
I saw the centre

where alfalfa stems begin their arc. I mended
the grassland, my darning needle witched,
plunged into earth six hundred
feet to water, to the Belly
River.

Song of Songs

Prairie knows her own beauty, silver willow, golden-
rod, her slopes thick with prickly pear, hawthorn,
meadow sweet, meadow rue, Orion in her deep
violet-blue haze, the shining arnica of her coulee.

To hold my quiet, in the noise
of oil rigs moving on the road a half-mile east,
on the gravel at the end of the lane,
to hold my quiet in silence, desire unable to vibrate

out from me, no pheromones to underscore
the call in my eyes; to hold this quiet,
it has to be filled with the sound of the '52 Chev
home from the hay field: the goat's flehming,
upper lip curled.

Winter sun would lift my face.
Ribbons of Sandhill Cranes would bind me
here, their necks and legs unfurled
as they gargle in the seasons with their rolling
garooo-a-a-a garooo-a-a-a.

He pulls his winter cowboy hat snug
over a Polartec cap held with a drawcord

He came in the house stripping off his clothes,
hung his overalls in the furnace room, set his boots to dry.

Hot bath.

Warm and dry Charl talked
of the axe in his right hand,
the line drawn in new snow
by the spade as he pushed
it ahead of himself to search
for the depression in the ice,
the cows' water hole in the Campbell
dugout. He spoke of ice over the hole
being insulated by snow,
how he went in right to his hip,
the way his clothes froze as he walked.

Then he spoke as if he were alone
if both legs (and here he paused)

it's deep there, cold,

if my concentration,

any disorientation,

to look up,

my hat.

Our place is medium-sized: the school board deals with sparsity and distance issues

This land where we till the soil, raise a few
chickens, pasture cattle, goats, horses, is all named
officially by number. The north half of twenty-eight
we call Johnny's, after the man who stacked his hay
and when he finished that load, let his fork slide
to the ground, slid down after it. The handle
entered him through his groin.

The northwest of four, the Nelson Place with the little girl's
grave. The northwest of seventeen where the Scot
built his stone house to overlook the Watson Coulee.
The steep depression that was Johnson's cellar, where we
found the calf, the cow worrying us during the rescue.
The old shed on thirty-five where we found the steer
dead behind the shut door, the same way
the neighbours had found Kistner in the house.

Those buildings gone now, bulldozed and burned.
And Matt bought the land of a distant relative
of my maternal grandmother. I imagine her cousin
thinking of moving on as he picked his goose-
berries from these bushes. As if the marriage
of Matt's son, not then conceived, would complete a circle

on this land. The Hudson Bay – where bunch-
grass, planted in rows, feels like waves bucking the truck.
The half section where Murphy and McFetridge built
one house on the quarter line and both filed their
homestead claims. The Fleck Place that Georgie calls
the Flat Place. Waldron's. Keith's. William's.
Rambo's: his widow sold their land to Matt. The team,
hooked to the disc, spooked, then circled back

as if ready to be caught, Rambo run over
by the disc. Kelts', where I look to the lights
on the tower to orient me as I haul grain
from the combine in the night, the swaths
curving around so many sloughs.

April 29, 1940 Matt and Lewsaw inked
their agreement for the southwest of three, Matt
promising to keep up the house and fences until the deal
was complete: 825 bushels of number one Northern
delivered to the elevator in town, one fourth
of all the wheat grown on the quarter each year

until the debt was paid. If he defaulted, cash payment
for all the undelivered grain, 75 cents a bushel. That
would be 3.87 an acre, the quarter section for 618.75
and a horse. That was the other part of the deal *one
bay gelding age 5 years, weight 1400 pounds, branded
quarter circle CE on the left hip* to pull the wagon
loaded with all their belongings, all their children. .

Roundup Ready ® canola

Jim says if he didn't use chemicals, his fields would be all
dandelions and other weeds, some of them noxious.
There's the pre-burn, the in-crop – hopefully only once – and
the desiccant pre-harvest.
He has ag advisors, GPS and weather monitoring.
He juggles degrees of tillage, crop rotation, seed banks and windows
of opportunity with rainfall, frost and his account balance.
He has a washer in his shop for the clothes he wears under his disposable
coveralls, goggles, hat and nitrile gloves. Otherwise the recommendation
is to wash these clothes alone, then run the washer empty
with detergent, the water level set for an extra large load.
Roundup® extended control product prevents weed growth in your yard
for up to four months. The label says to wash your hands after use.

Well water in a drought year I

Watering cows on section two in July:
take a mix of salt and mineral with you, arrive before ten,
before the cows start their serious drinking.
Fill the old Case with gas from the slip tank
in the '72 Ford, fifty-two measured strokes to the tank.
If you pump too fast the hose won't fill.

Water capacity: three one-thousand-gallon troughs
set up in a series with two twelve-hundred-fifty-gallon
tanks in the back of the Chev grain truck.
Estimate the water required, taking into account the temperature.
Use the stick to measure the fuel in the Case:
1.2 inches of fuel will run the tractor for one hour,
the generator pumps five hundred gallons per hour.
Don't run the troughs over.

Push the button on the right down; walk around
to the left side of the motor to adjust the gas valve.
Pull the choke out, open the throttle a little,
push the start button and hold it. If this doesn't work,
use the hand crank on the front to turn it over.
When it sputters, push the choke in and let it idle.
Engage the PTO, adjust the throttle 'til the needle on the generator
is in the green, switch on the generator, readjust throttle.
Make sure water is flowing. Recheck it's running in the green.

To shut down, switch off the generator, throttle back,
disengage the PTO, idle the tractor for a few minutes,
pull the button up, turn the gas valve off.

If something doesn't work call Dave.

Well water in a drought year II

Coyote inside the rail fence, around the well.
Paper in hand I follow Charl's instructions,
coyote keeping the wellhead between us.

Mule deer, whitetail, moose, elk, in the dry
creek bed, the brush, we're focused on water.

Thank you for calling the Farm Income Program Information Line

Please make one of the following *three* selections:

> Drought.
> Grasshoppers.
> BSE.

NISA: Net Income Stabilization Account.
Our office is open from 7 am to 6 pm central daylight saving time.
The final stabilization year is passed.

> He mutters in the bathroom.

This office has closed.
This is recording 306CT.

> The kids call it his office: *Canfax, Canadian*
> *Cattlemen, Grainews, Western Producer.*

TISP: Transitional Industry Support Program.
Your call is important to us. Please stay on the line.

> Phone tucked between shoulder and ear,
> I hang laundry, wash dishes, fold laundry.

Your business tax number please.
Your application is not in the system. It takes forty-eight hours from when you fax
it until it's entered. April 26th? This is only May 2nd. Try calling again in a few days
and if it's not entered, fax it again and phone in a week.

> He puts his boots on in the morning
> as slowly as he takes them off at night.

CAIS: Canadian Agriculture Income Stabilization Program.
Your information was received in December and has had a preliminary review.

At noon, quiet and slow,
he drinks his tea.

*It's been sent to a scanner – this is only June ma'am – and if it passes you'll
receive fifty per cent of the approved payment.*
*Depends where you are in line and how many cheque-issuing days they
have. First the office has to receive confirmation from your bank that you
have made the required deposit to a CAIS account for the protection level
you have selected. Some banks have special lending rates for CAIS deposits.*

Nothing that two inches of rain won't solve.

After supper, his chair pushed back,
two daughters on his lap,
his arm in practiced awkwardness,
he sips his tea.

*Yes, we have received the confirmation of your deposit. This is only August
and no, no cheque will be issued. You deposited only $16,377.57. The
deposit is short $10.*

Grasshoppers sit upright,
laying eggs,
their rear ends poked into soil.

*Yes, I have a copy of that letter informing you of the amount required. A
calculation error occurred. It is not our job to notify you of errors or of
deficiencies in your deposit. You want to add to your deposit? You will have
to discuss that with a supervisor.*

He posts the trot, the same lean in the saddle.

In this dearth some pack a .22 in their calving kit

What stubble there is,
is up,
open arms
to catch any snowfall,
hug its moisture into the earth,
loosen the banker's grip.

The music would be a cappella

When he didn't come in for lunch, the machinery running, she
shut down the loader tractor, the Supreme cutter/mixer/feeder,
called the RCMP.

Only his watch was recognized as the load of cut
hay was run off the Supreme's conveyer
onto sheets of silage plastic.

She wants to believe he climbed up to check the feed, reached
for a string he'd missed removing from a bale.

In the days after, she railed to her friends about his belly,
his center of gravity too high, berated herself
for desserts, his lack of exercise.

Caryatid and telamon by day (one of the kids might want
the farm), her shoulders shake only in the night.

Every day she engages the power-take-off, pushes that handle
up with her left hand, the blades turn, revs the tractor
to two thousand rpm with her right, with the loader drops bales
into the Supreme, two loan payments made on it.

In her kitchen over coffee she explored
where and how to move those twenty-seven
hundred pounds of cut hay, the need for a fire
permit, how long she'd have to wait for a snowfall,
how she'd gather his ashes.

Charl

He'll jerk his slack,
dally to the horn
where he'll rest
wrist on wrist.

Recognizing it for her own

Tomorrow we're freeze-branding numbers on their hips, back to the old way after cows lost double ear tags. Not that a brand would have helped us know who we found on the Fleck Place, the white curve of vertebrae and skull in the brome, the long bones, knuckles and hooves dragged away.

We'd run the herd through the chute, ivomec'd, matched coat colour, stub horns and switch length. Some we knew: 715 the black whiteface with a caesarian scar; the triple nickel with an offset patch of red around her right eye; and 846, the tan I'd seen looking a little off, then a few hours later near death. She'd lived, sloughed half her udder, toxic mastitis.

We fostered her little heifer to the cow Farley led home, a half mile north and a half east, his rope looped around her calf's heels, its head jostling along the ground, tongue out, its body pressing a path in the grass, in the dust, in the road.

Georgie made a jacket from its hide, slit it up each leg, underneath and circled the neck. He peeled it off, pulled it over the foster baby's head, laced it under the belly, the back covered, loose flaps of hide over its legs and brisket, two tails swinging behind.

The calf placed in front, off to the side in case the cow staggers

The range cow on her flank, both heels lassoed, will strain,
two legs protruding from her swollen vulva.

When the calf's head is found folded deep to its left rib,
my feet braced to nudge with fingertips the loop of chain
over ears and snug into mouth, after grunting
realignment of calf with birth canal, I will couple
the arc of my pull with the calf's curved path,
force, with cow's breath.

Charl will shake some slack in his heeling
rope. I'll slip the loop from the cow's hind feet.
The cow will be agile in her anger – I'll stumble,
the horse will ignore the rider's heels, or green,
will shy at the rope – the cow, head lowered,
will rub me into the earth.

Cause of death obvious: rib cage crushed

The pathologist will turn the body in his hands, search
for contralateral lesions
to chain-link bruises from left wrist to inner elbow,
find another track of chain fainter on the other forearm,
neither encircling the arm;
turn the unwashed hands in his,
note short-clipped nails, half-moon nicks,
blood, meconium, dried around cuticles, between fingers,
smeared up the arms, over the left shoulder,
on the left ear, hair dried stiff around it;
sniff, smell iodine-based scrub, amniotic fluid.

He will turn the body in his hands,
read history in healed wire cuts,
pick up the left elbow,
test the joint against the scar tissue,
marvel at the survival of radius, ulna,
carpals, metacarpals, innervated phalanges.
The hand that led,
the lead hand.

The pathologist will turn me in his hands,
scrutinize, wonder what he might have observed
from a distance,
how I moved my body,
how my body moved.

But if this poem is to be all happiness and light

There is so much I cannot say. I'd crossed
the Watson Coulee to see if the red brockle-
faced cow had had her calf. Deep in buckbrush
I saw it wet, already knowing mother's tongue.
I lay in prairie wool to photograph this
glacier-divided hill, its scooped curves
where moon rests early in her rising up that deer path
in the ice-age draw. I climbed that trail, circled
down to the hollow on the slope where
a rock's animal face is aligned south for winter sun,
not chiselled, no mark of stone on stone.
Where grasses eddy by that rock, see the poem
on my notebook pages blown by the wind,
held by binding. Read of rock-warmed night,
morning: flooded, sun-licked as the deep
violet-blue of silverleaf psoralea.

I had known the finesse of his tongue

In the barley dust Charl coughs up phlegm,
spits. Hell, he works outside, spits all the time
and not the lean-over-and-let-it-dribble-
spinning-a-web-of-mucous spit.

With the tip of his tongue pressed
to bridge his teeth, he builds a pressurized
trap, propels his spit in a synchronized
elegance of lips, tongue and breath.

Why doesn't he hork sounds from his larynx,
shape them into words with that same
exuberance.

I turned to him –
his hands, his arms, occupied – he spoke
I'm working on this clutch then I've got
brake lines to bleed.

II

When grasshoppers strip her naked

and coyotes ululate in the night,
Prairie rises on her haunches,
shakes her bloody rags at the moon.

Not me,
not any more,
no bloody rags.

Downner cow

The bellow, the swing of head,
scrabble of front legs, the breath,
points north.

Coyotes uncork the belly south,
magpies follow
and if the season's right, blowflies.

In the hospital room I opened
my eyes to blues, dull gold, white,
cranes flying behind the morphine

pump, across the moon: a swath
of fabric I'd tacked on the wall.
And Cousin Matt with yellow tulips.

This alkali slough between us

Now when days are short I bake potatoes in the evenings.
Bins in the cellar hold a winter of suppers.

In May, Georgie drives the tractor, one of the kids behind
on the planter drops potatoes cut for seed into long furrows.

Come fall, after the frost, before the ground is frozen – I seek
this balance so the skins are hardened for good keeping,
the potatoes don't glitter in the light then rot
in the bin – Georgie does the tractor work and I toss
the potatoes to dry on the south side. I have to cajole him
to keep the tractor moving, help me gather potatoes into pails,
haul them to the cellar, the seed kept separate. The pace
quickens when the kids come home from school
and despite Georgie's predictions

we are finished before dark. I wrap these potatoes hot
from the oven in a soft cloth, tuck them against my pillow.
I bathe with heated water in a basin, scrub with soap, sluice
fresh water over my body. In bed my neck, damp from my hair,
on the warmth from the potatoes. I move the bundle to my feet.
Later, on my side, cradle it. When I hunger in the night

skin and flesh are warm. When I am not needed to listen
for children in the day or in the night, and that will be soon,
I will press my body to the earth, make a print in withered grass,
outline my shape with rocks I heat with fire, build
effigy of woman sleeping.

Bedded in that warmth, when I shift my body in the night
stones will tumble with me, their heat pressed to my feet,
the hollows behind my knees, they will mark my shoulders,
girdle my waist. When I hunger in the night, my back
to the earth, I'll turn to Orion, to the genesis of stars.

The raven was an iridescent black

Coyote started where the body was
tender then hollowed the core.

The pathologist sliced tissue
with fine precision, stained
sections, pondered slides,
sucked his teeth in indecision,
counted his shortlisted
rule-outs: eenie meenie, icka
bicka, one potato. He changed
his left glove, smacked his other
fist into it, held my ovary
to the light, a one-hand
repeated toss, catch, spinning it
in the air. Signalling a changeup
to his colleague, he made the first
throw in a lively game of catch.

For ten days I was left
to believe I had ovarian
cancer: this was good.

I'd been praying for
an anesthetic death. I was given
no replacement hormones –
a post-surgery blood clot precluded that.

Through all this I'd been handed
piecemeal, as an avoidance
of discussion, a new vocabulary:
dysmenorrhea (painful menses)
dysuria, dyschezia (painful urination and

painful bowel movement, respectively)
chronic pelvic pain (all words I already
knew but this term included the pain
down my legs, the pull of adhesions
and their tearing apart)
dyspareunia (painful sex). This was the word
they were most anxious to give me, even
spelled it out. They didn't want to hear
how the pain lasted
into the next day and the next.

A spicule of bone in my throat

Charl used to grip the edge of the bathroom sink,
rock his body, a standing push-up, work for breath.
Asthma. I'd hoist whichever child had to pee,
then step by when he leaned in. I never knew
if he knew we were there. When he was well
enough to flood a rink, play shinny with the kids,
I stood watching before I put my skates on.

When his lungs were bad, he could wear jeans
with a twenty-eight inch waist over heavy long johns.
The farm not so mechanized then, Georgie and I
pailed grain to the cattle, forked the cut hay
in the bunk-feeders, kept track of the boys; Charl
running the tractor some days with Bronwen sleeping

in her seat. Zoë not yet born. Evenings he'd tell me
how to manage without him. Nights
I'd wake up if his breathing was quiet or
the quiet was because he wasn't beside me.
Hearing his nebulizer, I'd roll over
next time I wake up I'll see if he's alive.

I wonder if he couldn't walk over this ground again
when I wasn't well, couldn't acknowledge his fears:
raising four kids on his own, how he'd keep the farm
books. Perhaps he couldn't consider scaling his life,
his farm management, the way he'd told me to.
Maybe somewhere within he was hoping.

As if that absolved him, made him not complicit

When I called home from the airport Charl knew
but didn't tell me my father had died, said later
your sister told me not to.
By the time my flight was in, the funeral
was set, no time for my children to attend.
No question of Charl having time,
he's a busy man. I drove without him

to both my surgeries. First one
ovary, big as a saucer. Blood
and fibrin bound it to my uterus, glued
ureters, bladder and loops of bowel
together. People don't speak

of this blood, where it grows, what
it strangles. My left ovary
tied to my side, a hardball,
a shiny nickel in my pocket.

We had our own memorial for my father.
He's not buried, not released from my sister,
his ashes are in her closet. I never saw his body,
my body parts in stainless steel, my
tissue thin-sectioned under the microscope,

stained, not buried, instead
incinerated, or in formalin, photographed
for some textbook or reproductive medicine
class. The doctor exhibited me to residents
before the second surgery *here, proof that*
a woman with endometriosis
can have children; see the cervix pulled
to one side by the scarring. Tell them
how many children you've had.

Bluestone for algal bloom

With no estrogen, with this sleep deprivation,
my thoughts are stones. Their dust works
into the bark of my hands and dries
my mouth. When I focus to remember a word –

badger, clitoris – I wander through the headlands
where my stoneboat's been off-loaded, where I find a Rock
Dove who nests in my buccal cavity – her squab will fledge
from my tongue. I brood

about my drooping eyelids. All this is about aging, my loss
of language, memory, the tipped planks worn smooth,
their grain a relief of contour lines.

My stones are meadowlarks flying
from my body, Yellow-shafted Flickers,
their tapping muted as they forage in the earth for ants.
In late summer my erratics are in clusters, chokecherries

gobbled by waxwings and coyotes. What's left
can be stripped from the bush after the frost,
bone and astringent fruit
uncoupled.

I am a marker for elevation

Cold ankles down.
Downhill the chill is to my knees,
my thighs, 'til in low spots I'm wading
chest deep, holding my arms above it,
deep in the coulee I'm swimming. I'm in
over my head with no base
to stamp my feet on. Cold
undresses me.

At night in bed I hold my book, see my pulse in my wrist

Erin pleaded for the black range cow's death, the unborn calf
dead, lodged, the cow down. I gave the cow an analgesic, drove
away to check on other calving cows.

The next morning the suture line smooth, the cow licked
her foster calf as it suckled. I tell you this so you know
I don't rush to deliver death. I won't tell you how
I struck her to make her stand, lurch into the trailer.

I've shown neighbours how to cradle their dog,
raise the vein. I've held the foreleg, rested
my left thumb along the side to steady the blood.
I do this to spare them both the .22's clap
clap (the second to make certain).

Lucy was held by my voice. With a grip
on her elbow to occlude her blood, I rolled
my hand laterally to make her vein accessible.
I must have put the children to bed first for a nap.

In the evening, on the phone, long distance, I explained
all my reasoning to Charl. He has always said
there was nothing else to do. In all these years
he has never said *I understand.*
I forgive you.
Let me hold you.

Effigy of woman sleeping

Coyote gleans fruit from the ground,
on hind legs eats from branches,
claws dirt, chews shoulders
of carrots, his scats flecked with orange,
the seeds of apples, pears. The heady
redolence snuffed out.

I made myself use that fabric

The bed is pushed over to the wall under the window.
The apple crate and old chair, with reading lights,
are not flanking the pillows.

He's worried

about pieces of fabric laid on the floor,
quilt squares in patterns of blues, orange reds,
greens, and purple with windows, their sills
alight with sleeping cats, pears, red roosters
with golden combs, all the colours linked
by yellows: plaids, tawny, cheddar.

Those cranes flying across the moon.
What changes if he, up in the night, skews
scissored cloth, looses colour?
What if he, up in the night, climbs under
fragments, shatters the pattern into chaos,
the elliptical glide, steep climb of Cliff Swallows?

What if he injures flying geese? Their wings
will bruise his night. What if geese
escaped from the mosaic are swans,
or cranes? (He doesn't think of them.)

What if all the slips of fabric are words?
What of the quilt he sleeps under now,
what is written in the nights?

I need long fibrous lines

No, I am not brave. Where the sun rises,
sets
on this grid of roads, tells me the season.
The correction lines keep true north, kill
the unsuspecting.

(I was on an outcrop on a sidehill.)
Old woman, tacit, showed me my daughter
to divulge the need that I be –
I stopped praying for death.

I picked up my pencil,
gathered my disparate parts,
what was left by coyotes.

For mending I gleaned split barrel staves
from the long-abandoned Stauffer yard
(the sisal disintegrated when I tried to scavenge it),
from my garden, corn husks,
from Prairie, willow branches soaked supple in rain water,
fallen swallows' nests, flax pounded into slubbed linen,
snagged horse hair from tails flicked on barbed wire,
native grasses, forbs, sedge, harvested in bloom, reaped dry,
chanced-upon feathers,

for joinder spittle, thistles, nettle,
hippomane from mare's afterbirth, dried, ground,
brewed in tea to rekindle bodily links
for elasticity of earthy tug.

Within the dovetailing, merge, mesh, plait,
the splicing, warp and woof,
was the pause, Breath.

Dislodged by blue

I'm riding the buffalo on my plate towards the blue
drops that made it a second, caused me to choose it

from the potter's shelf. Blue underclothes, camisole
concealed by grey jersey, Levi's worn to light blue.

How else can I entwine my fingers in the dusty
curls on that terrible hump of his shoulders, know,

but hold myself as if unaware
that he will pass under the blue, those flecks,
other buffalo behind him.

Four gates to the fields east of the Watson Coulee

If the gates had tied shut, with a couple wraps for leverage
I would have pulled them taut,
picked slivers of weathered rope from my hands. As it was,
I leaned into the gateposts, slid wire loops up and off.

The pathologist will turn me in his hands,
puzzle over narrow linear criss-crossed bruises,
vertical marks from my axilla, faded before my clavicle.
He will turn my body in his hands, compare
left, right.

Poplars were the shell, we the blood on the slough

We went looking for the missing
cows: a grey, a grey brockle, and a red.
By the end of calving I'd been reading
every grey's number, looking
for 819 and 946; several days read 948
with the field glasses, circled sloughs and rocks
to be closer, to see clearly
through long hair obscuring her tags.
250, the red checked as calved,
had disappeared since.

We went looking on the west half of nine,
thought they might be in the bush, watched
for prints, fresh pats, black flurry of feathers,
moving shadows or bones not yet bleached porous.
Nothing, even around the big slough
merged with the dugout, both still
full so late in the season.

                              August sunned
the water, his back, my face. Poplars
blocked the wind.
His shoulders, tall slough grass, shallow slough.
Hazel, the black tips of her ears delineating,
her tail ruddering, her path on the knoll.
We leaned on water, into jonquil light.
He spoke of ducks, of saving this stand

for winter grazing, of water levels
and we remembered the grey
had drowned in the Campbell
dugout last winter, the grey brockle had

died of pneumonia in the fall, and the red,
Farley had found dead in July,
struck by lightning. He'd brought
her calf home, fed it with a bottle.

All recorded in Charl's breast
pocket notebook, not transferred
to the official book for all to read.

Prairie's had a two-inch rain

She unbinds her breasts, ends her silent keen,
blushes with pink bee-plant, wolf willow.
Horned Larks ride her sway

of grass. Blackbirds, Yellow-headed, gregarious
at her springs, Red-winged flirt their wings open
with each cry. Prairie clasps Orion

between her thighs. Charl knows the owl
from a distant bull, from a Mourning Dove.
Some nights I have no arms. His weight

on my inner thigh turns my femur to a crow
bar, opens me – my latch unsought.
Cotter-pinned, my body stirs.

Some nights he breathed up all the air

I can sit at this wooden table now, two leaves
in it, a variegated hoya grown from a slip from Marg
sprawls in bloom, taking up a quarter of the space,
the Congo letters from my father at the other end, a wall
of books behind me, in front a bay
window facing east, another south.

I can sit here to write now that
Red-tail has made his final plunge, his right
wing spread for lift, his left bound to his body
(a quick bandage to hold it still, stop the bleeding),
his feet, his eyes, clasped shut.
Later I could see his fractured bones were imperfectly
aligned, his testicles bruised, his lungs

dark with blood. This is behind me now
as I write, oddly, about sleeping
beside Charl, the way his breathing changes.
Red-tail needed to be past the shock before I could set his wing.
I rolled a towel for him to rest on.

Charl's muscles move when I breath-kiss, rub my cheek, along his back.
Days later I cut through muscle to open Red-tail, know his viscera.
Now that my bloody masses have been scraped out – left
an immutable yearning
and a matting together of intestine and bladder
into a daily question of how, if, they will work –
I've had to re-gather my desire: strands

from the mare's tail, knotted taut inside my body,
carry the vibration of touch from here to here
to here. If I'd known I wouldn't have prolonged

my breathing, Red-tail's breathing with warm fluids.
I wouldn't have had the surgery. I'd have flown to Newfoundland
or just come home, expected them to live with my pain.

Charl could smell my pregnancies, knew, but waited until I spoke.
All that irrevocably behind me.
No matter how tender he is, and his touch is always gentle, even
now I am a dark bruise. I gather myself, hold myself, to sleep.
This may be what he couldn't bear: my shaking afterwards, my drawn up knees.

He was changed when he came home from that horse meeting:
in his sleep he said *oh my God* and *how was I to know?*
During those unending months when he didn't touch me
(I never really slept), his mare colic'd. I said *it's surgical,*
shoot her, we live too far from anywhere to save her,
wanting to say *I love you* in the heat of this. He didn't want
to hear me, said *this isn't the time.* Later I showed him the twist
in her bowel but right then how could he believe me?
He didn't want to hear her heart was a jackhammer
pull the trigger give me the gun. What could I know,
my hand on her skin where her blood curved over her jaw?

I don't speak of what we do, what we say afterwards,
whether the northern lights flicker, about the leaves
on the wayfaring bush outside our window, if the covers
are in disarray. A few lines sketch a chickadee – she's
fluffed up against the cold – on my cup filled with water beside
our bed. Some nights I am inadequate for him, this

                                    spills over into other nights.
I love the feel of his body, my arm first outside the covers, my hand
on three layers of quilts, their colours in the dark in the moonlight.
The feathers on his bowed head were ruffled. Red-tail. Before he died.

Long after or before, my face the other way,
I'm prone, my forearm along Charl's back.
The scent of hoya wafts into our bedroom only in the night.

Some nights by myself on a blanket on the floor, heat billowing
from the register, Hazel, her ears up, looking at me from the chesterfield.
Other nights I've lain south of the caragana, never mind the temperature,
whether I'd catch my death of damn foolishness.
I turned from his warm back to switch on the light,
write these lines, the words flowed into me
how he spent his days
         no time with his horses.

When I cut into Red-tail, his feathers took flight. His smallest feathers,
smaller than you'd imagine, floated on the water in my cup.

Guttural sounds in our throats

I pocketed two stones, the size of ovaries – they
slap my body as I run three gravel miles of February.
Hills later his tongue softens the block in my mouth
from petrified wood to burr oak, planes off long curls.

III

In the year of the plague of Biblical proportions: August fair entries

Impaling grasshoppers with pins does not kill them. They leap about the kitchen anyway, Frankenstein ballerinas, spot their heads on pirouette. In the microwave, hoppers tendu derrière, a terminal pose: their bodies, fragile, break easily in the hand. A fresh bevy audition, jeté into melted dark chocolate; a brief stir then scoop and lift with tweezers. The hoppers kick their legs into first position – chocolate to die for – a tempting crunchy sweet with strong dark coffee.

A slight microwave mellows a grasshopper polka to a waltz; a waltz into jars with crushed garlic, fresh dill. Boiling vinegar and salt solution cinderellas their costumes: they bloom from dull brown greens to rich mahogany, bellies amber. Redder eyes peer through the glass. Wipe the jar rims to ensure the seal. Pickle for ample time. Serve with lightly salted whole grain crackers, well-aged cheddar – a still life.

Grasshoppers swan dive through melted white sugar, rise to a decorative plate. Promptly manoeuvre antennae into an extended position, nudge legs into the desired stance. In time hoppers stand with stunning detail, organic earth-tones highlighted by glaze, lovely with an after-dinner mint.

In one grand battement the 'e' from hope is gone, the dance described. Rise to the challenge of keeping back legs attached for anatomical correctness. Remind guests to pluck, discard these legs in earthenware bowls, as the spines will scratch the mouth, catch in the throat.

Our breadboard and table came from her kitchen

Light falls in slow horizontals on fields
of long swaths with herringbone corners
where the combine turns on the dime Charl catches
in his mouth as it bounces off the taut harvest,

the same dime Sadie, his grandmother, bounced on quilts
stretched on wooden frames. But that was winter work.
Nothing could be balanced on the backs of chairs needed
by threshers when they crowded into her kitchen.

Farm kids are their staple

for Gordon Henry Stauffer
June 11, 1889 – November 6, 1917, Ypres

When recruiters come to the high school,
all epaulettes and smiles, promising
adventure, education, jobs, don't tell them

that prairie kids monitor computer data for pressure,
density of bales, watch the knotter indicators behind them
while straddling the swath, yes on corners too, all the while
listening to the Wurlitzer and answering the two-way radio.

Don't tell them how these kids
know the sound of the equipment, do their own repairs,

how their eyes find calves hidden in buckbrush.

Don't tell them how these kids catch their own horse, ride
through the herd, move a particular range cow, coerce
her into the trailer, get the door shut. Don't tell how they spot
the rusted wire of an old fenceline, lead their horse over it,

and, when that's what has to be done,
they slog through snow to their thighs,
shoot their own horse.

That Christmas Eve she'd whispered *no, you* saw *me singing*

for Margaret Gould Hutchings
March 28, 1909 – December 25, 2000

Charl's auntie read all the names and dates as she walked with me at her elbow. Most of the family burials had been in the last few years and perhaps the weather had been too harsh but she had never pressed to attend interments. She had stayed at the church with her husband. She knew only where the older generation lay.

Except Elizabeth. She knew where she was in her family plot, her marker obscured by the tree her mother had planted; no grandparents or even distant cousins in this then-almost-empty cemetery. In this land without bush or tree and them not long here from Nova Scotia. That 1920 train ride: thirteen children and the two sisters-in-law.

The men had gone on ahead, their journey separate from the women's. Sisters, brothers, cousins – some we didn't search for, knowing they were buried elsewhere. Graham had come home, was buried on the prairie. His war bride will follow him here, her chiselled name and birth date holding her to her word. Now he waits. She waited for him during the war, unsure at times if no word meant that he was gone, what gone would mean.

The two widows, we knew they would lie beside their husbands. We found her eldest sister, her husband, their grandson. Charl's parents – we talked of their unnamed daughter, her place not marked. A second brother, his wife, their daughter-in-law, their stillborn great-grandson. His grave made the family five generations

here where we breathed, in the unseasonably warm autumn afternoon reading the cemetery map, headstones as landmarks to find her ground. The dimensions stepped off, she gazed from her place to her sisters', her brothers', her cousins' near the unruly tree.

From her house where she'd set quart sealers between the two-by-fours of the walls to keep cool, from her house where the Scottish woman hired as help said *peace, pairrrfect peace* in the morning when all the children were off to school, from her house, her brothers' farm had been three miles south, the cousins' home place a half mile west of there, two of her sisters on farms north of town, and a cousin north of the hills and east.

She was always tranquil, her tears easy. That afternoon in the cemetery with all her years overlapping, she was dry-eyed, serene, her knuckles too large for her veined hands.

I can still see her braid swing across her back

Mornings Erin drank black coffee.
No Tim's out here on the prairie and when she visited
civilization in Red Deer, Tim's was undermined by Charl's brew.
But it was really all about the tea we drank
after meals, for the examination of the calf record book,
over Scrabble (we renamed it *lovat* after Farley proved it was a word).

Erin laughed.
When she'd really laugh she'd wave her hand as if to fan herself.
We'd laugh harder and she'd say *what? what?* amidst the mirth
of Georgie's bear stories, complete with compass directions, gestures.

She must have put the kettle on during the phone call,
when she saw my body sag, didn't ask who or what,
hot tea with warmed milk. She gathered up the cat food,
pails, headed for the goat pen, evening milking.

The evening I first met Erin, everyone else away when she arrived,
a calf, warmed, coaxed to drink colostrum, greeted her in the porch.
She was here only minutes when we carried him together, back
to his mother, waiting where she'd last nuzzled him. We checked
that calf all summer, mothering up the pair when he was far from the herd.

Erin lost her brand-new-bought-for-this-job work gloves that first evening.
She wore holes in my extra pair that summer. August
I found hers in the brome grass north of the house, faded.
She wore them, drove back east.

We weaned in October. That calf never learned to drink from the waterer.
I remembered Erin's dark braid as we lifted the calf up and then away.

He said *sit here to feed the baby,*
in the blue chair, that's what it's made for

Irving is here not just in the storytelling,
in the way our babies slept with us,
and how the kids lick their ice cream bowls,
he is in this house, this kitchen, in the grout lines.

Of the five, only Irving's two eldest have first
names without a history. He named
Matt for his brother, his grandfather, an aside
to the Matthews and Charleses alternating
through the generations of eldest sons
and it was Cousin Matt who came from Edmonton
a day ahead, brought Irving's ashes here
to this kitchen where he spooned them into the urn.
The ashes spilled everywhere, like Irving did,
more volume than you'd expect.
We breathed him in, laughed as we brushed him
onto paper, funnelled him in,
quiet as the wax melted for the seal.

The interment was held at the family reunion,
years after Irving's death. He'd died
soon after Zoë was born: we'd waited together.

Marg and I walked, she spoke of euthanasia,
the right to decide, I of Matt,
Irving's brother, how he would have chosen –
the abyss after his years caring for Edith.
We talked of legislating death, of analgesics,
side effects and prayer. This was the time Matthew,
our eldest, tipped the Buddha off the shelf,
broke the head from the body.

First crow sighted March 10th

Georgie rushed home for binoculars when he sighted
a bear in the Watson Coulee, across
to the east. Blood pressure rising, he closed
one eye, focused on… barbed wire rolls
stacked in the fence corner, ready to spring
out from hibernation, receding as the crow

flies, oblivious to survey stakes pried out with crow
bars, to be put to other use – the line fence already sighted,
built. Drooping wires marked the fence where the spring
thaw had heaved the pickets, left them hanging across
the wire, suspended by single staples, others rolled
out where the wood had split: a struggle to close

the gate. The skunk wasn't kept out of the barn by the closed
door, went in and out like a cat. When the rooster crowed
the skunk stamped her feet while the cat food rolled
into the dish. Georgie, bushy eyebrows up as he sighted
the raised tail, retreated to the seed shed across
the yard for his .22 bolt action. ISA brown pullets, this spring's

chicks, would tempt a mother skunk's spring
appetite or a weasel's. Difficult to keep the henhouse closed.
He wouldn't shoot a weasel but when the skunk strolled across
the yard, Georgie fired one shot. Something to crow
about: his long wait, the meticulous sighting
down the barrel, the way the skunk toppled, rolled.

The smell wasn't that bad 'til his dog rolled
on the carcass, carried it around the yard. Spring
uncovered a mangy coyote frozen under snow, sightless
excrement of winter; but its eyes weren't closed,
they seemed to watch the cleanup crew of magpies and crows.
Georgie patrols his routes, his pen travels across

the squared page – his records are survey stakes across
the years. On his calendar a roll
call of species: gopher, bluebird, crow.
Each year he chronicles those firsts of spring,
location and species journaled in the closed
boxes, a special notation for every weasel sighted.

He nudged his dog across the truck seat. Off to the spring
in the north field, he rolled his window up, almost closed.
A crow cawed. Georgie was hoping for a meadowlark sighting.

Allan discerns Psalm 29: 6

Allan and I have different stories about his first day of work. The preacher's
kid from Burlington tells about the caesarian section – Yankee war bridle
to manipulate the calf's head *push the calf in, gotta get the head comin'
right*, the cow bulging her rumen into the incision, his hesitation *jump
up on the side of the squeeze, lift the calf*, Charl up the side too, hooking
handles onto chains double-half-hitched around front pasterns. The pull
to free thighs lodged in hips (we'd washed the shit off the crossed back
feet), the yellow wheelbarrow overflowing with calf.

My story, from early in the day, on pasture, the truck motor off *what
do you see?* His hands flighty birds, I mmhmm'd until the *oh* of his
first birth. I don't include his hands in the telling and neither he nor I
elaborate on the unfolding or the sun burning off the morning fog.

Our later stories merge: the beep of his watch reminding him to pray, our
silence, my separate listening; how we predicted the phrases of Charl's
curses through the calvings, those stories as mixed as the breeding –
despite the chess game of cattle not across the fence, not kitty corner,
where there was grass and water, the neighbour's bulls, last year *in
flagrante delicto*, their get in fetopelvic disproportion to our cows; we
guessed the parentage of the over 120 pounders: Maine-Anjou for the
blacks; the tans, Charolais. Each story with an interlude: out of cursing
distance, we'd keep Charl's red shirt in sight, its body billowing, sleeves,
bent at the elbows, flapping, urging his horse in pursuit (we'd landmark
his Stetson, retrieve it); one red sleeve forward, back'n'up, and down
to the horn to dally, then Charl reining, Teddy's back feet under his
haunches to pull the cow down, for us to re-arrange, pull the calf.

Somehow, live birth after live birth: head back, backwards, leg back,
twins. Allan saw nothing dead until he'd fallen in love with the brown
of Prairie's throat, her collar open to the sun that dried the calf, its head
twisted under a front leg. The open eyes echoed the crescendo of his
prayer nailing flawless imperfection. Selah.

While he waited for the school bus

The neighbour kid plugged a coyote,
.22 long,
roadkill deer for bait,
a calf dead from pneumonia when that was gone.
Twenty-five bucks for a frozen coyote,
didn't have to skin it.

Russian thistle tumbled down the fenceline,
caught, loose, caught, pushed before the wind.

He waited in Prairie's cold distillery,
narrowed his eyes at the weasel's black-tipped tail,
the moon low in the sky.

When the sun rose east-northeast
and he'd moved his jackknife
from his insulated overalls to his jeans,
he picked off gophers 'til he saw
the dust plume of the bus.
No carcass to hang on the fence.
The same weasel, black-tipped tail,
white fur shed for brown,
slipped around the old wooden granary
where the kid stood his gun
butt down on the two-by-four sill,
clip hidden above the lintel.

Mom

I've gone to Joel's
to boil deer skulls
back before 11:30
love
Farley
ps turned the oven off
didn't know how
long
you guys would be

The early hours his, perforce the late evening mine

Come morning he'll brew coffee, eat almonds and figs.
Now he reads, his legs stretched down the bed, feet together,
covers neatly folded on his bare chest; in the cold,
a fine woollen undershirt, long sleeved. Even in the heat
of summer Charl buttons his cuffs around his wrists.
His eyes close – against his weariness, not the page.

Bronwen speaks to him as if he were awake
our basketball game is at 5:30 tomorrow.
He says he'll be there. She knows he'll stand against the wall
in his black cowboy hat, moving his comb from his left
to right pocket, and back again, marking which team
gets the ball when the play stops, saying nothing
when he notes an error.

Beside the slough south of the house
on Georgie's scarecrow, meant to protect the ducks from foxes,
a crow perches above the waving shirt, listens, head cocked.
Hazel stretches her legs, her paws in a small circle, sighs back to sleep.
She knows the sound of the boys, young men now, coming home.
As they walk through our bedroom – a door to the east and west –
Matthew bookmarks *No Great Mischief,* sets it on the ladder-back chair.
His hands empty now, Charl turns on his side, pulls the covers

around his shoulders. The house deeply quiet, even Zoë
settled, Charl truly sleeps: his leg sentient, sentinel,
flung across the open prairie of the bed.

Charl

As immeasurable as black up down of wings:
with him, without him, not touching, touching.
Crow, raven – unknown in their overlapping
seasons – will (perhaps) soar.

Grief submerged with her brilliant feet, tucked up in flight

The hay cut, the Northern Shoveler lost her eggs to crows.
Too late in the season for another clutch, she dabbled, swam
in small circles, stirred the muddy slough bottom, her wide-tipped bill –
olive green speckled with black – long, not absurd as she drew in water,
combed for seeds, insects. The brown of her body was mottled, her head

streaked with dusk, her eye just above the water line. The mare
flank-watched, shifted her weight. She had come into her milk, her teats
beaded. Outstretched – her foal poised – her neck, her limbs extended
with each surge. His shoulders angled through her pelvis. I see why

Charl thought I foaled like a good mare, swift, resilient – it seemed easy,
this separation, her velvet calm. The colt's hocks still in her open canal,
his body in the torn amnion, he swung his head, lifted himself sternal;
she had the same momentum, turned to clear his muzzle. Then

her forequarters rose almost straight up, like the Shoveler from the water,
from her nest, her legs briefly trailing. The mare, circumspect
about her feet, turned to mother, whicker; the duck's quiet *chooka
chooka*: her young had been near ready to pip. The colt's fetlocks strong,
the soft caps on his hooves feathered now, his suckling a prologue

to her after-pains, her cleaning: the placenta, now afterbirth, expelled.
Our afterwards, our days, passing – gleaned as they are for joy, they
are like the Shoveler's bill, tending to orange along the cutting edges.

The function of shear pins

His silence baffles as much as any talk. Buckled
to the load of our days, we live with the badger
of again – our muteness, our words

brace, peck and quarter. When Zoë finishes high school
I'll be on this horse of marriage as if riding after freezing rain:
muscles tensed to lift me in the saddle.

The angle of the wings, the set of his mouth

We're cutting with two machines. Charl opened this field and he makes the first round of every slough – he can see the distance, know how far he is from the fence, the bush. At the northeast corner a crow (it's summer) circles the haybine with easy flaps, his beak dipped to turn his eye downward, see if we will touch. Charl catches me up, his gear ratio different. I knew it would come to this, me pulling out of the swath at the corner, him going by. The bird, shiny as he loops away over the swaths, as if a raven, soars, harassed by smaller birds. On acute corners I swing in tight counter-clockwise circles, don't gear down except for low spots heavy with alfalfa, sweet clover or reed canary. Like a hawk the black bird follows the haybine, hunts mice as if he were a raven summering here.

I publish a poem in a journal. Charl reads it, says *you call this a poem?*

When I first knew him, he read his combine manual

Later he would read to our children, laugh out loud,
read himself to sleep – *read, Pa, READ.*

He taught me how to open and shut gates: round turn and two
half hitches; flip the loose end of the chain outside so the cattle
can't lick it open; watch the metal arm doesn't come up too quickly,
shatter your jaw; lean *into* the post to loosen the wire,
don't push *up*, the loop still tight. He gave me time to struggle.

Crabs, stem up, in lines on the cutting board – John Drinkwater's
"Moonlit Apples" on a smaller scale. Matthew had learned that poem
...the apples are laid in rows...those moonlit apples of dreams.
Charl, his mouth puckered, set the fruit aside; not yet the season
for a beard, his face – moustache and a few days' stubble – legible.

His father had read him *Smokey* years before.
Working in the field, I saw him stopped, not labouring
for breath. Later he said *I couldn't get out to open the gate 'til Gzowski
and Michael Ondaatje finished talking.* Months later he picked up my copy
of *The English Patient,* read it, demanded others like it *no junk, I haven't time.*
Now he's outgrown me, specifies authors, titles, bought himself a Richler,
Cocksure, when he went to Edmonton, to the lung specialist.

By then I hadn't been photographed for years. Now the children shoot me,
my face blurry in every frame.

Their lovers are like you

Pussytoes cushion your head for sleep on prairie wool.
Rough fescue for your itch. Foxtail barley tied to girdles
of many-flowered asters. Thread-leaved sedge couples
its spermatozoan shadows with moist willow sloughs
and big bluestem dances its turkey-foot seed heads

in intricate patterns. You don't understand
how it happened: Prairie has daughters.
Their beaus hold northern bedstraw and owl's clover
to their downy cheeks. These lovers can't resist –

they chew the root of wild licorice, touch the curved sticky
bracts of yellow bright gumweed. They must stop
to pick *Stipa comata* from their feet and legs.
Scratching their balls, they find them
speared too, the pointed seeds needled in,
the long awns curled.

Thank you for *Seed Catalogue*

With Robert Kroetsch, and Roger Tory
Peterson, and Vance Jowsey and McLean's
revised and expanded *Wild Flowers Across
the Prairies*, and *Poisonous Plants Agdex 666-2*,
you could grasp the prairies, almost, ok you couldn't,
but they could remind you if you knew,
if you were, through it all, still, gazing
at three-flowered avens, still startled by Horned Larks.

Art Spencer, Special Areas man, knew, not book knowing,
first pussy willows, spots to pick saskatoons,
chokecherries, knew the grasses, old school sites,
teepee rings, buffalo wallows. Art could key any plant.

He's dead now, the knowing in fragments.
Men, who think they're familiar
with what they think is theirs,
figure they can school Prairie with a D9 cat, push
the Great Horned Owls to other land.

Jim ran broncs all over the prairie. He knew
some, a different knowing: catch-colts and grass,
knew not to get a phone. He's in the home now, gone
soon enough, the knowing locked up.

Knowing the locked-in sameness, weather
socked in, drizzling mud, impossible
that it will ever end. It doesn't.
Neither does the drought, cold, heat,
like working cattle at the chute, more cows
in the pen, one more in the alleyway, one
jumping, smashing the top poles of the corral.

Farley works the back, has a flow
of cows ready for us to vaccinate, preg
check. He's always playing basketball,
new knowing, the kid's growing
his own. Moves with his horse, jumps, intercepts
a pass, drives for the basket, runs his haybine,
changes sections, guards. He knows the rock
piles, the fences, the low spots, the roads. He knows
years of drought, grasshoppers, the runoff
of heavy rain. He knows his .22, picks off gophers
at thirty yards without a scope, leaves them
for migrating eagles. His telephoto lens ready to shoot.

IV

The jars are translucent blue, the lids glass with zinc rings

Farley came so quickly that I pressed my left foot
into Charl's cupped hands, his fingers interlaced,
my other foot in a nurse's hands. The push
of birthing passed through his hands up
into his shoulders, down his body, through
his hips, his legs. In haying time

the air filled with clouds
of dragonflies, I heard a neighbour say
you got good help when you married her
and I heard the reply *it wasn't worth it.*
Now what, now that the children are grown?
Years ago, that night he drank, not a lot, enough

to talk *I would only marry to have children*. I fold
the years it took me to hear this, my stretched arms
a measure of the cloth I unpin from the line,
fabric pressed by wind, preserved with all its scents.
The creases of stars and diamonds will be revealed

later. I read that people with severe forms of psoriasis
are likely to die younger than their peers. I hope Charl didn't
read the article, didn't give his body permission. His affliction
has settled into arthritis in his neck, his knee, the top
of his sternum. There's a joint in his breastbone,
some flexibility through his heart? I'm searching

for the nomenclature of our bond:
clevis – curvilinear, the arms not parallel, it doesn't lie
flat, only the holes in the cusps line up for the bolt;
noggin – the horizontal timber between wall studs;
cushla-macree – pulse of my heart. Growth arrest lines

cross the epiphyses of the long bones of our marriage.
I plunge my hands, up to my elbows, in the rawness
of these stoppages, pass this through
grain-cleaning sieves, wonder what to store
in glass sealers, what to compost,
if it could come to nourish what sustains us.

This year's pullets are red. The axe, black feathers
on its head, leans beside the henhouse door
where we go through with grain, water, pails
of carrot and potato peelings, fruit pulp from jelly-making.
Charl tells me where to stand as he chops the ice to make
a new hole for the cattle to drink from the dugout.

See the path the axe head would follow if it came loose
his left hand at the end of the handle, his right, near the head
to raise it above his shoulders, slides down the smooth
wood, his hands together at the end, for the impact. He shapes
a dish, wider at the top, the sides steep, a small passage

in the bottom for the water to well up, fill the bowl, his beard,
his moustache, glazed with ice, by late winter his mouth
a dark pit, his tongue a pendulum of concentration.
Each morning the water hole is reopened. The channel
in the bottom grows gradually larger until, like a pelvis
with softened ligaments, the cervix thinned to nothing,

a body could pass through, a reverse birth,
a return to the water. I can see no depression
in the earth where Matt buried his stillborn daughter.
We helped him firm the earth over Grandma Edith,
and we tamped his grave, knowing what he'd expect.
The children with their smaller poles. The same ones

they used to help us set posts for the windbreak.
Farley in kindergarten then, nine in the cemetery,
trying to understand the echo in his hands,
reverberating up into his shoulders,
down his body, through his hips, his legs.

I need shirts in plum blues, raspberry, sage, soft Levi's

In Edmonton for the diagnosis, we stopped on 105th just off Whyte Ave. for ice cream in waffle cones. The woman started in on how he was too big to be carried, shouldn't he be in school. All this happened after he had finished kindergarten, told me he'd figured things out *it's like cows and horses but with people it's private* and before he was eleven, still too lean, running the big feeder, recording the pounds of feed in each bunk, backing into the shop, before he was nine, learning to rake hay, not pushing the throttle to full rabbit.

We were living in the big house, Grandpa Matt's, while ours had bedrooms added on. Even now Farley can't bear to be inside for long. I'd set him on a blanket in the October sun. He learned to rate his pain one to ten, once asked when it would stop. The girls played make-believe. Matthew carried his pillow downstairs, refused to go back up until Farley could. I see now that he could have had his bedroom without breaking his word when we moved back into our house. Charl's mealtimes grew shorter, he worked late, but when we figured out the doctors here weren't helping, it was Charl who took him to Texas. Georgie wrote him letters about the pullets laying, rounding up the ducks and geese before the slough froze, the snow.

Farley home-schooled that winter, sustained by light coming in windows, and colour. His red ball cap on backwards, wearing Wranglers, his long sleeve button shirt with red flames, he'd hook the heels of his black cowboy boots on the chair rung, white Texas longhorns and stars on the tops, a narrow red stripe on the sides, red stitching on the toes. This winter I see redpolls in the Siberian crabs, see them feeding on seeds on the ground, their caps solid red, their breasts marked with quick strokes. He must have coloured them that winter he wore his poppy-red pencil crayon down to a nub.

Alumroot was in bloom

A doeling outdistanced a coyote across the swaths,
ran into a slough. All was still
until a willow moved as if a brief wind stirred it
or the bush were shaken for fallen fruit.

I signed my letter to my daughters
I press my cheek to yours

Wash me yourself, you know the lavoir
where water flows from the ground.
Wrap my body in unbleached linen,
bury me deep on the north
of three, on the prairie west of the slough.
Tamp the earth,
put back the mat of buffalo grass, sage, yarrow.
Search the headland, the fencelines. Lodge
rocks in a Celtic cross aligned with the four
cardinal points, for the solstice of summer,
winter, the equinox of autumn,
spring, a spiralled triskell on each arm.

The partridge will nest in grass, sheltered in the hull of my ribs

Those bales Charl is surprised the calves eat so well in their cut feed, are filled with dried flowers, the scent of honey – bales of pathos, the beaten trail to the open mouth, the unmarked track to the bone. The small white flowers, so beautiful in the bales, are hawk's beard (if you are reaching for your wildflower book to prove they are yellow, I'm telling you the tight buds in the hay are white, not the golden they might have become). That spring every time Charl tried to seed, the land was too damp. Soon it wasn't a flush for the rod weeder but a stand starting to flower. This was breaking: the crested wheat and brome, the sweet clover and alfalfa in resurgence, the hawk's beard muscling in. He cut, baled, then seeded late, swathed the stand of grain before the frost for grazing later in the fall.

I'm heading home now, my rudimentary quest to see Breath – the raven holds it in her bones and her wings imprint the snow as if a grizzly scratched towards the centre, leaving no paw prints. The sun's twin dogs, their muzzles to their master. Lost in possessive adjectives and confused pronouns, I seldom travel in such silence. I dreamed I was in a corridor where I could open a locker and know. I hesitated before a door, heard breath sounds, controlled as only Charl can – a warning that the wire around the louvre encircled his trachea. All I could do was move on. Death would come with knowing.

When Farley and I found Princess, the old mare, down, Charl's leg was in a brace, his femur held together with screws (a collision with a ram, but that's a different story). He used his crutches for his first outing, rode with us in the truck to the field. We talked about the angle of the shot and how the mare's star skewed the perception of that imaginary X, the diagonals from the inner canthus of her eye to the base of her opposite ear. Blood ran out her nose. Farley said it didn't bother him, he'd done what had to be done.

People put a distance between themselves and the dead. Even if they wash the body and lay it out on the covered table or on a board on the backs of chairs and the dog leaves to go to the neighbour's until after the burial, there is a distance. The body is washed with a quiet reverence, a certain awe, and laughter. Zoë's hair will fall forward. Bronwen's mass of curls will be in a bun that holds itself without pins. Matthew will know how things should be done and Farley and Zoë will spar.

When the time is close, let me wear the slubbed linen smock, stretch along a tree branch like the porcupine we thought was dead until she drew up her paw, humped her way back and down. I'll breaststroke through poplars, switch grass, sheep fescue. Ammonites will rise, sink, as they siphon water, their spiral shells lustrous mother-of-pearl, buffalo stones. Breath will shear through all my body. Old woman will draw me under her prayer shawl, antelope hide lined with wild flax, fringed with drop-tine sheds, buttoned with skulls of deer mice, badger claws on her shoulders.

I'd walk that path back to wakefulness

You move with purpose through your exercises, counting each
aloud to ten, your new femoral head smooth in your old acetabulum.

Each meal you ask if I want bread. I don't eat wheat. You agree
no, you don't eat wheat. After meals you explain *Nancy*
says if I want to wash I must use hot water and I must rinse the dishes.

I'd always dried while I told you about my school day.

I'm piecing a quilt, trees on a light background, not in neat rows,
rather scattered, overlapping, saplings growing near
the base of mature trees, some leaning, starting to topple.
I bring this fabric in October, March, October. When I visit

this time, Nancy is away, leaving us together. March you simmered
in your rooms in Nancy's house, wanting to go home. Now
October, photo albums over tea, you rearrange time and
I'm anguished by the cuckoo out of sync – you wait

for no bird as you push the hands. I've thawed
blueberries and you stop reading to me the same poetry book
you read aloud straight through yesterday. You want
your blueberries plain, not with yogurt, you never could abide
junket or anything like it after you had typhoid as a child – those same words,
that same inflection I've always heard. The fabric is spread all over
the table where you eat your fruit. I'm wondering when you will leave me

blueberry prints through the light background, a trail through the trees.
I'm perversely hoping.
I'd set that path with hot salt water.

When I came to the conclusion, knowing
Farley would agree, I didn't wait

Afterwards the scab from Crow's chest sat for weeks,
an upside-down dried-out mushroom on the back
corner of the sideboard next to part rolls of bandage, tape.

We'd been working in the shop when Roxanne called.
Farley made the pick-up, an easy capture in a hedge,
dropped an old towel over the bird.

He held Crow for most of the bandage
changes, the bird suspicious of anyone different.
In a few days the softened scab worked
loose, exposed a hole in the sternum's keel
where a pellet had rebounded out of bone. We took
serial photos of the granulation, measured
the wound's need for cleansing, rebandaging, against
the inevitable

disturbance to the right wing. Unwrapped
it would have hung as if attached by tenuous
soft tissue so Farley held it folded to the body.
Crow switched from eating softened kitten chow

to tearing every bandage, stripping
away his own feathers and flesh,
his brachial plexus avulsed,
his wing no longer
part of himself.

If there is to be no reconciliation

Don't try to give back love:
drop it in Sounding Creek,
a green twig carried downstream.

I wore each of your kisses as the owl wears death –
with no expectations, with a thousand expectations
of love.

If you want your kisses back,
I will gather them,
every one.

The Common Loon I carried, downed
by an early storm, from the field to open
water where it dived to feed before it flew –
I knew to avoid its slashing bill;

the Bohemian Waxwing, healed with
two days of arnica, yunnan and aconite,
ate Nanking cherries from my fingers –
his crop filled, I released him into December.

Your love has never nested in my body.
Come summer I'll travel to the Neutral Hills,
your Northern Harrier kiss lives there – I'll know her
by the healed tibial fracture.

The Great Horned Owl, his right wing
dried, twisted backwards, flight
feathers splayed, the inner coverts
turned outwards, the humeral fracture
compound and comminuted,

beyond any intramedullary pin,
any Kirschner wire – for this kiss
I offer his down and a handful of earth.

His flight muscles wasted, I could
have curled on the shelf of his sternum,
my back pressed to his keel.

Unflinching in my hands, his
weightlessness diminished
when he withdrew his will.
It happened so quickly, as if
he died of my intent,

or resolved to preclude me.
He still holds me in his knowing, his look
with no judgment, fear, or blame, no peace
to make with God, nothing to forgive
or be forgiven. I see his eyes now as he
watched me through the cut-out handle
in the box while I made the preparations.

The sound of milk modulates as the pail is filled

Black bird in Prairie's March sky over the Nubian
in the milking stand. I look up, think *crow.*
If it's larger *a crow that's close*
or a raven further off.
How to know the distance, my cheek
on goat's flank, her rumen roll a distant thunder.

In drought years we can see the parallel ruts of given roads

It was two weeks later when Bronwen asked
how does Deadstock get Lady to heaven? We talked
about horseness, the horse's body. Now that would lead us

to compare species, the way a mare postures, pees,
a stallion's curled lip as he snuffs up her pheromones,
how his back feet come off the ground, sex and love

and readiness. I thought I was randomly choosing
quilting fabric, carrying bolts to the counter. When
Harriet – it's her store – said *that's a different combination,*

I saw in the greys, the browns, chestnut and rust:
the grey partridge, his rapid wingbeats and low glide.
Charl's hands are like my father's. I had answered all

Bronwen's earnest questions as best I could, listened to her
four-year-old self. She was almost seven when her grandpa
died. I remembered. She had her time alone with him.

Last summer she and I walked through strands and strands
of gossamer that spanned paths, roads, floated free above
the grass, silken bridges left by spinners kiting in the wind.

The kids took the sifter to the sandbox years ago

I'm baking with butter and molasses, the ginger,
cinnamon and cloves gorgeous on the brown rice flour.

I wrote 11:56 at the top of this page, subtracted four
from the baking time, wondering how much later
than the gingerbread the girls would be home from the dance.

I'd planned to do the baking earlier but I was reading, writing
letters and was ready for bed when I remembered I'd promised.

Come morning Farley will open the water for the cows, pail
grain, fork hay to the horses. I'll start the calf-load cutting,
work from the notes I wrote warm in the tractor in sunshine,
Charl saying which bales to use, to put the greenfeed in first.

Farley is heading back after chores. He finished his ag economics
between periods of the Montreal–New Jersey game.
I want to give Charl every detail, want him to see Hazel
on the chesterfield, her ears up when she hears her name,
me, here in this kitchen eating frozen Evans cherries
at the stove to warm my back. I want him
to know the wind is keening around the house,

to come home, catch me up,
tell me about his cousins, his auntie's
funeral, how the family grieves.
I'm wondering how I would mourn for him,
if he would mourn for me.

Crow

lands in the dead
poplar, mocks me by name as I hang
laundry on the line, jeans in six sizes,
all those socks in pairs in the breeze.

Rosy everlasting above their mat of woolly leaves

Matthew works his math equation, glances up,
moves the tractor ahead, pulls a part-
load of bales into position for his father
to set more on. He works through
the next step, shifts down as he hauls
through the rough. His load topped,
he heads to the yard, his books
between the hydraulic levers and side window.

He gears up on the flat-fell seam of road allowance,
driving between rows of fence posts and barbed wire
that stitch fields together – he's pounded in
posts like these, stretched and stapled the wire,
replaced posts broken or heaved out by frost or heavy rain.

He passes the wooden snowplough,
pieces fallen to earth, wood felted into Prairie,
part of the tilth – sees his great-grandfather, coal heater
at his feet, clear grass to feed cows in a year of early snow.

He ponders school in the city, how he'll long for Prairie
where poplars grow slender, smooth skinned.
How to find such a woman to love him.
Girls at school talk only of moving away.
A university woman, with her own studies, she could live
in the gravitational field of Prairie. He'd gather
wild roses with her in that light before dusk.

Her spelling homework about the various sounds
of *i*: shiver, spiral, thirdly

Zoë heard bleating, found the doeling's
kids buried in straw, not mothered.
She dried them with soft cloth, nestled
the two in a rag-lined box, their long
legs folded.
More stubborn than the goat, she
milked her, bottle-fed the colostrum,
took the cleanings out of the pen.
She told her story with joy, her ending
quiet *I left the dead one outside the gate.*

This year, two gestations:

when Tom's bulls visited (repeatedly),
when our bulls were turned in with the cows.
In the morning of the day we preg check the heifers and young cows, I reach
in first then Farley. Last year frustrated, now he picks up the cervix, palpates
the uterus, the ovaries of open cows; finds the stages of their cycle in the tone
of their inner horns; discerns the incomplete tract of a freemartin. The
pregnant girls are well along: he can feel the buttons, ballotte the fetus gestated
as long as he had been

> when the pinto mare broke my ribs. Charl had been
> holding her head for me: he wanted to know if she'd slipped her foal.
> Shoving him forward, her hind feet cleared the post behind her. Against
> the plank fence, doubled over I heard
> *what the hell's the matter with you?*

> That Lucy dog rode in the truck with me to the hospital; every filled
> crack in the road a shaking, the railroad tracks an explosion in my chest.
> Women in the hospital corridor *she must have been working; I saw them
> carrying her boots.*
> I slowed my breath,
> tried to help the drugs stop the contractions.

In the afternoon Farley goes first: checks their tailheads for hair loss, reads
through their rectums. My body language, the speed of my palpation, not
clues – he knows
I check twice before writing *cull* on the record page.

Older cows, even their open horns down over the brim of the pelvis, the cervix
large for me to grasp and retract the uterus. My shoulder inside, my fingertips
just brush those calves from Tom's bulls, deep in the bellies. Farley's better at
this, the strength of his hand, his wrist, the reach of his arm: he's grown, his
autoimmunity long quieted, his kidneys spared. He turns
his hand to the side, to the middle
uterine artery, the turbulence of blood to the calfbed
a fremitus in his palm.

The heft of my woollen turtleneck, the hand
of goat down next to my skin

           Driving west through Manitoba with the gnarl
of oaks native in Erin's pasture on my mind: whole fields
of sunflowers, all their faces bowed to the east and they stay bowed.
They didn't lift with the rising sun and the *Hallelujah* I heard was

sombre. I imagine Erin's laugh when I tell her we both forgot
my books, the ones she borrowed a year ago July, the time she asked
why I stayed and we talked of kids, of prairie, longing and love

and what if.   The palmate lupines I'd set out volunteered
the following May, their first two leaves closed fists – on a hunch
I didn't root them out of the flower bed. The yard needing more
than its annual trim, I mowed around gaillardia, buffalo beans
and coneflowers, left the wild flax too. Charl loves

that morning blue with his coffee.   He and I were quiet
beside the acorn seedlings under the burr oak we'd planted,
then as we considered where to move them, our sleeves brushed
one against the other –
a compress of wild bergamot.

           Coming clean across Saskatchewan, I'm home
to prune the raspberries. I work on my knees
to cut out all the old wood, bare my hands for each
cane's last berry of the season: on my tongue, they are the ending
whole half whole descending tones, and with them, earthy,
that fleeting lift of muscle: an eclipse of self by the wilderness
of Breath, hinged with the insistence of the blood, the soma.

Last spring, with wire, I portioned twins inside a cow:
their hair and hooves sloughing, I pulled them out piece
by stinking piece – head, forelimb, hind leg with hemipelvis –

until she was empty. The smell had passed through
my double-layered shoulder-length gloves. I gave her medication
and she staggered off as we gathered all the oddments.

I watched her on the prairie. Her back arched, she strained,
whirled to sniff each scrap of afterbirth, anxious
for a calf to lick into a certainty of life: the minor scale,
the muscle riff.

Let me rub your hands with pumice

Turning, I see your outline in the trees,
in the negative space –
you on your horse, as if you were
there. I feel your mortality,

felt mine when you backed the trailer
to the chute where I leaned –
the shirt Farley had outgrown
and my old Levi's moved my body
while I wondered if we would ever both be

in love, at the same time, with each other.

I walk the ripe hay for the lost
calf, hope for reconciliation,
for a decision – not grass to open,

close over us, one then the other.
I search for you, find me.
My path circles a slough. You ride
this field your rope in your right
hand, reins left, come down

from your horse.
Let me wash her sweat from your thighs.
We are older. Let me try again
to wash you, turn your body, in the water.

I see my love more clearly from a distance

From the bustle of the kitchen he's a smudge of blue, then jeans and jacket
where he pushes barbed wire down to straddle the fence. He crosses

the headland into grass he planted this spring with the 1940 double disc
drill converted to seed twelve runs, each with its own species, fourteen inches
apart each pass around the section. He crouches beside Russian wildrye,
Altai, his cowboy hat worn through on the folds. When he stands to examine

the northern wheatgrass for definition, I see frayed threads on his collar.
The alfalfa is stripped to bare stems. The barley is no better: the beards
and leaves eaten, paired grasshoppers bow the unfilled heads of grain.

Charl looks for the brighter green of reed canary that he seeded separately,
engaging and disengaging the drill, circling here and there. I thought he was
crazy until he explained *low spots, reed canary tolerates standing water.*

He's sweating between his shoulders where I kiss him in his sleep.
If he turns from the grey-green sage, the healed sutures on his lower lip
will tempt my tongue.

Notes

"Who can tilt the waterskins of the heavens?"
The title is from *Job* 38:37.
Buffalo grass – *Bouteloua gracilis* – is also known as blue grama.

"Song of Songs"
The title is from the *Song of Solomon* 1:1.
A flehmen response, or flehming, is an upward curling of the upper lip
to help draw scent into the vomeronasal organ.

"Our place is medium-sized: the school board
deals with sparsity and distance issues"
Like other land named after the previous owner, we call the land the
ranch purchased from The Hudson's Bay Company, the Hudson Bay.

"Well water in a drought year I"
PTO stands for power-take-off. The PTO shaft transfers power from the
tractor to the piece of equipment being run.

"The angle of the wings, the set of his mouth"
When using pull-type haybines, only one machine is in the field during
opening: the haybine is driven counter-clockwise around the field. All
subsequent passes are clockwise.

"The partridge will nest in grass, sheltered in the hull of my ribs"
Drop-tine sheds: Sheds are the antlers lost annually by animals such
as deer; tines, the projections on the antlers, usually point upwards.
Occasionally, on one or both sides, a tine will point downwards: this is
called a drop-tine.

"In drought years we can see the parallel ruts of given roads"
Given road: an expression that I've heard used in southern Ontario for a
road that has been returned to nature.

"This year, two gestations:"

The cow's uterus consists of a body, which is fairly short, and two horns.

A freemartin is an infertile heifer born twin to a bull.

Buttons, or more formally, placentomes, are the sites of attachment between the fetal membranes and the uterus in cattle.

Open horns are the horns of a non-pregnant uterus.

Calfbed is a common term for the cow's uterus.

Acknowledgements

My thanks to the editors of the following publications where versions
of some of these poems have appeared: *Best Canadian Poetry in English
2011, Contemporary Verse 2, echolocation, Eleven Eleven, Prairie Fire, The
Prairie Journal* and *The Society.* Also to Don Domanski, judge of the
2009 Banff Centre Bliss Carman Poetry Award, and to the sponsors:
The Banff Centre, Prairie Fire and McNally Robinson Booksellers.

I am grateful to the Alberta Foundation for the Arts for financial
support for preparation for and travel to the 2010 Thin Air International
Writers Festival in Winnipeg and to attend the 2009 Piper's Frith.

My thanks to the Banff Centre for help to participate in the 2007-08
Wired Writing Studio.

Warm thanks to Hilde Seal and her Aunt Elinor Maddock for sending
me to the 2009 Sage Hill Poetry Colloquium.

Thank you to Shannon R. White for photographing her pressed plants
for use in this book and to E. Bronwen Gould for all her help with this.

My gratitude to Jan Zwicky for her insight and patience throughout the
editing. Thanks to Kitty Lewis, Alayna Munce, Cheryl Dipede and Brick
Books.

My thanks to John Lent for that pithy consultation at Red Deer College
in May 2007; and to Robert Kroetsch for his encouragement, for books
and for pointing out the root of a poem.

Special thanks to Seán Virgo.

My gratitude to the people who read and discussed poems, keeping
me company, long distance: Karen Lee Lewis, William Caton, Heather

McKend, Rob Taylor and Erin Rubert. More thanks to Erin for her hospitality, her inspiration and for shepherding me around Winnipeg. Thanks to Judy Hodge for helping me to identify prairie plants and for the copy of *Common Native Pasture Plants of Southern Manitoba*.

Many thanks to my family for all their support and for checking technical details.

These poems were written *for* these people – some of them are now *in memory of*: "Well water in a drought year I" for David Gould; "While he waited for the school bus" for Joel Kelts; "Their lovers are like you" for Robert Kroetsch; "I'd walk that path back to wakefulness" for Grace Woolcott Birkett; "Let me rub your hands with pumice" for Charles Gould.

This collection of poems is dedicated to the memory of Rick McNair.

Nora Gould writes from east
central Alberta where she ranches
with her family and volunteers
in wildlife rehabilitation with the
Medicine River Wildlife Centre.
She graduated from the University
of Guelph with a degree in
veterinary medicine.